This journal belongs to

_____

THE JOURNEY OF THE SOUL

Hidden in the symbolism of the early tarot are legends and myths from ancient times. *The Baddeley Tarot* reveals the meaning and pattern behind these stories, linking them to once-forbidden esoteric wisdom. The cards draw upon imagery with origins deeply embedded in the mythological journey of the soul that weaves through life and beyond.

The images in this journal are grounded in the spiritual systems and philosophies of the time in which tarot first arose. The illustrations reflect a style and technique inspired by the Renaissance masters. Multiple layers of meaning are interwoven in the imagery to create a rich tapestry to guide your soul's journey through the complexities of life.

I have interpreted the images based on my study, experience and insight into the cards. Now, I invite you to do the same. This journal is a sacred space where you can enter, explore and expand on your tarot journey, and make the interpretations your own. As you record your readings and add your reflections to these pages, you are creating a valuable resource. Color the images and include associations, feelings, outcomes, sketches and anything else that brings you closer to meanings that are true for you.

Yours in tarot,

Jake Baddeley

At first sight, the major and minor arcana may seem like an eclectic collection of meaningless imagery. As we become more familiar with these images, their history and their mythology, the tarot begins to speak to us in a clearer voice — the allegory is revealed and endowed with more specific meaning.

Your relationship with tarot may start with simple interpretations. Over time, it will deepen into something far more personal and, eventually, give rise to nuanced and multi-layered intuitions and insights into these mythic, archetypal images.

YOUR TAROT JOURNEY: ALLEGORY AND TRUTH

The adage "a picture is worth a thousand words" is very true of the tarot, as libraries have been filled with discourses upon its imagery. Whether crafted by chance or design, tarot imagery contains many layers of meaning, leaving simple, single interpretations inadequate or constrained. Their symbolic nature invites contemplation and evolves with our understanding. Herein lies the beauty of the tarot and why so many have been drawn to it throughout the ages.

Although we know that tarot evolved from fifteenth-century playing cards, there is no written explanation of their allegorical imagery. With no set text as a reference, many diverse theories about the meanings have arisen. As an artist interested in symbolism, I wanted to create a tarot deck that reveals the true meaning of the cards. Still, like anyone else, I could only guess at what the original tarot designers intended. This led to many hours of searching and research for clarification, eventually uncovering the early tarots that seemed closest to the original intention and the secrets of the allegory. On the journey, I discovered many fascinating details of tarot history which I have incorporated into the design of *The Baddeley Tarot*. There is much for you to explore with the tarot, and this journal welcomes your reflections, insights and more.

MAJOR ARCANA:

The Greater Mysteries

No explanation is known to have accompanied the original tarot. No interpretations of the card meanings have come down to us through history. This is why there is so much diversity in the explanations offered by tarot scholars and users today. There is also a surprising amount of agreement about meanings among tarot enthusiasts. Interpretations seem to have been passed through the generations by word of mouth or intuitively understood from the symbolism. Thus, we cannot 'know' the meaning of the images just as we cannot prove that one meaning was intended. We can, however, guess and with experience, intuition, insight and knowledge, this guessing can become more of a certainty.

Although I believe, as many do, that there are precise meanings to these images, intuitively reading the symbolism is an excellent place to learn or improve one's understanding of the cards. Reading images is a learned skill — it is like reading words, but different. It is a flow of associations, an index of affinities, a web of meaning. With an image, meaning can be layered upon meaning, one interpretation may contradict the other ... and this is okay as both are relevant aspects of the image's construction. A picture can hold all at once.

Tarot imagery can aid contemplation. It can unlock thoughts and feelings and act as a guide or template upon which we can hang our ideas. The images are a mirror in which we see our opinions, our prejudices, and ourselves. Name what you see and see what you name.

THE FOOL

THE JUGGLER

THE HIGH PRIESTESS

THE EMPRESS

THE EMPEROR

THE HIEROPHANT

THE LOVERS

THE CHARIOT

TEMPERANCE

JUSTICE

FORTITUDE

THE WHEEL OF FORTUNE

THE HERMIT

THE HANGED MAN

DEATH

THE DEVIL

THE TOWER

THE STAR

THE MOON

THE SUN

JUDGEMENT

THE WORLD

MINOR ARCANA:

The Lesser Mysteries

Tarot's Minor Arcana are divided into four suits which are linked to the four elements. *The Baddeley Tarot* diverges from the association commonly used today and harks back to an older period. Historically, each element is assigned particular qualities.

In this way, each card acquires a particular character and flavour. The associations of the suits build into a web of correlations adding layers of meaning to the cards and facilitating their use as divinatory tools.

Each card is also assigned a number that represents a planetary sphere and the deity who rules over this. These fit together naturally as they are symbolic ladders to Heaven. The planets are arranged in the Ptolemaic order — an arrangement of the planets and stars that has its roots amongst the earliest of civilisations. It follows the logic of form unfolding from emptiness. This extends the web of correlations into astrology and the macrocosmos.

With experience and practice, your interpretations will grow in depth and clarity, taking on ever more subtle meaning as your skill with the tarot grows.

THE SUIT OF SWORDS

The Element of Fire

✦

Qualities:

Warm, Dry,
Bright, Passionate

ACE OF SWORDS

TWO OF SWORDS

THREE OF SWORDS

FOUR OF SWORDS

FIVE OF SWORDS

SIX OF SWORDS

SEVEN OF SWORDS

EIGHT OF SWORDS

NINE OF SWORDS

TEN OF SWORDS

PAGE OF SWORDS

KNIGHT OF SWORDS

QUEEN OF SWORDS

KING OF SWORDS

THE SUIT OF BATONS

The Element of Air

✦

Qualities:

EPHEMERAL, WEIGHTLESS, MOVING

ACE OF BATONS

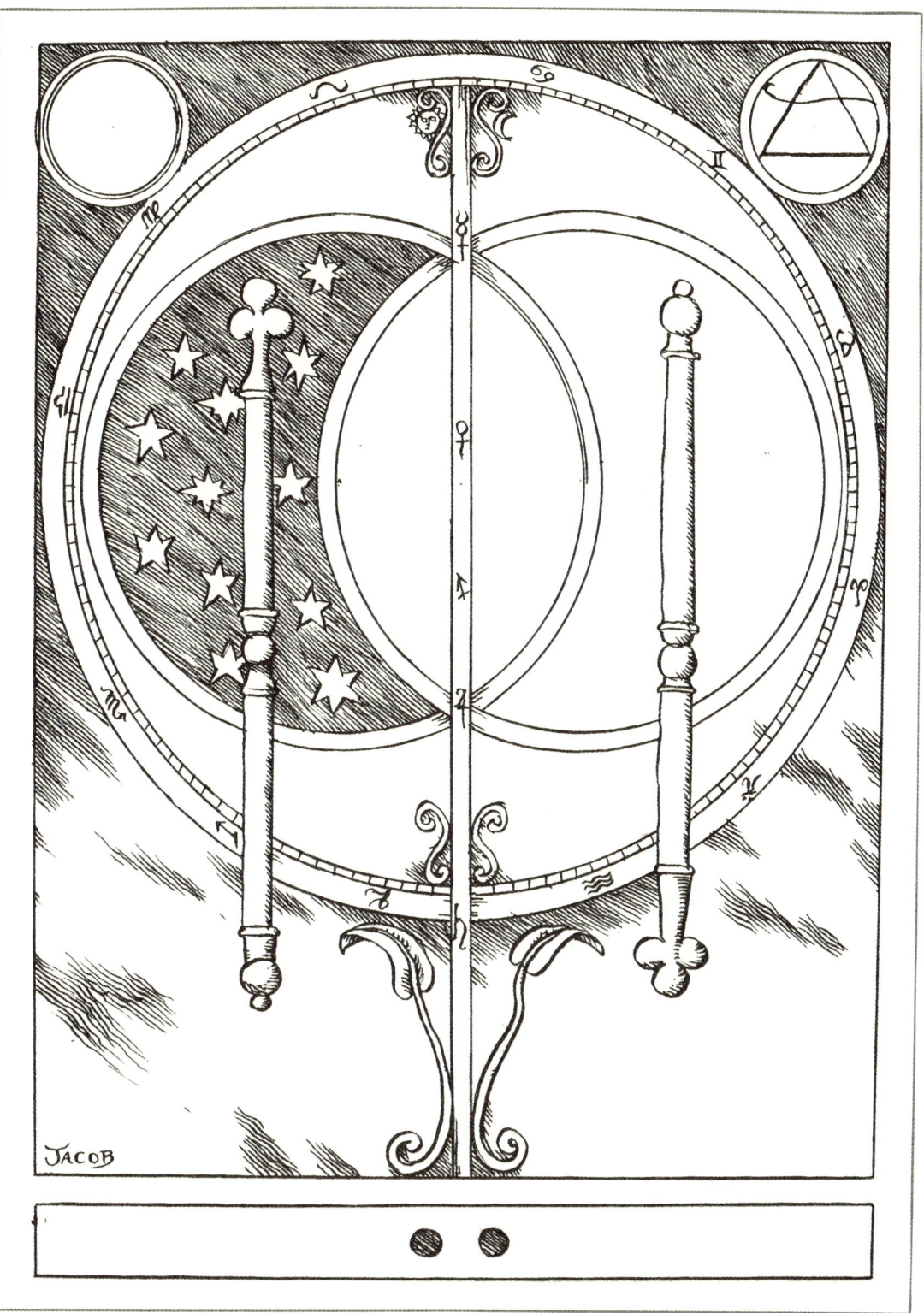

TWO OF BATONS

THREE OF BATONS

FOUR OF BATONS

FIVE OF BATONS

SIX OF BATONS

SEVEN OF BATONS

eight of batons

NINE OF BATONS

TEN OF BATONS

PAGE OF BATONS

KNIGHT OF BATONS

QUEEN OF BATONS

KING OF BATONS

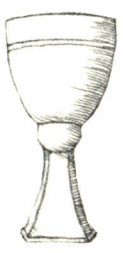

THE SUIT OF CUPS

The Element of Water

♦

Qualities:

Cool, Moist,
Smooth, Purifying

ACE OF CUPS

TWO OF CUPS

THREE OF CUPS

FOUR OF CUPS

FIVE OF CUPS

SIX OF CUPS

SEVEN OF CUPS

EIGHT OF CUPS

NINE OF CUPS

TEN OF CUPS

PAGE OF CUPS

KNIGHT OF CUPS

QUEEN OF CUPS

KING OF CUPS

THE SUIT OF COINS

The Element of Earth

✦

Qualities:

Hard, Heavy,
Stable, Abundant

ACE OF COINS

TWO OF COINS

THREE OF COINS

FOUR OF COINS

FIVE OF COINS

SIX OF COINS

SEVEN OF COINS

EIGHT OF COINS

NINE OF COINS

TEN OF COINS

PAGE OF COINS

KNIGHT OF COINS

QUEEN OF COINS

KING OF COINS

About the Author & Illustrator

Jake Baddeley has been painting and drawing for as long as he can remember.

After studying art in London, Jake travelled around Europe, eventually settling in Holland, taking up oil painting. The Old Masters, such as Rembrandt and Vermeer, guided him from the Rijksmuseum and Mauritshuis walls in the Netherlands. Jake learned all he could about Dutch painting in the Golden Age and synthesised these techniques with the ideas of C. G. Jung, the role of the unconscious and the archetypal divine feminine.

He became interested in the tarot due to a long fascination with symbolism and ancient myth. In uncovering the hidden mysteries embedded in the tarot, he felt he was slowly being initiated—whether he liked it or not—into something of great significance and value.

With Blue Angel Publishing, he has collaborated with Lucy Cavendish to create *The Great Goddess Oracle* and *Blessed by the Goddess*, and his stunning original artwork appears in the *Dream Journal* and *Goddess Journal*. He is also the author and artist of *The Baddeley Tarot*.

He now lives with his wife, son and cat close to the sea, writing and painting whenever he can.

For more information please visit
www.jakebaddeley.com